Harry Furniss

Australian Sketches

Made on tour

Harry Furniss

Australian Sketches
Made on tour

ISBN/EAN: 9783337191900

Printed in Europe, USA, Canada, Australia, Japan

Cover: Foto ©Andreas Hilbeck / pixelio.de

More available books at **www.hansebooks.com**

Australian Sketches

Made on Tour

BY

HARRY FURNISS

LONDON
WARD, LOCK AND CO. LIMITED
NEW YORK AND MELBOURNE

CONTENTS

Some of these impressions were first published in the *Melbourne Argus*, and others in the pages of the *Windsor Magazine*.

Running the Quarantine Blockade

AN American humorist tells a story of a man who was lost at sea, and who swam and swam for an interminable time. He gives the most graphic account of the feelings of this man whilst battling against the waves, and then says: "At that moment my friend touched something hard—it was the United States!" Now, that belated

GOING TO QUARANTINE

American could not have had more difficulty in touching the United States than I and other passengers arriving last week in the good ship *Victoria* had in touching Australia.

We had had a splendid passage all the way from London, and no illness whatever on board. The passengers did not leave the steamer at Aden, as there was no time; and the *Victoria* arrived at and left Colombo with a clean bill of health. After a run of ten days, we reached Albany. Before boarding, the pilot—who, by the way, turned out to be harbour-master and major-domo of the whole port—asked the usual question, "All well aboard?" and being answered, "Aye, all well," unsuspectingly stepped on deck. As soon as the anchor was dropped, the port health officer came alongside and informed us we were in quarantine. We soon learned that Aden had been declared an infected port, requiring the usual smallpox quarantine of twenty-one days clear. The steamer having only been sixteen days out from Aden, five days' quarantine was ordered. The

OFF TO THE WEST

weakness of the regulations was made evident by the fact that the steamer had a clean bill of health from Colombo. However, all the passengers for West Australia were taken off to quarantine, including the unfortunate harbour-master.

Days before we arrived we had pictured to ourselves a rush to the goldfields as soon as we had touched Albany; and immediately on entering that prettily-situated harbour I made the sketch, "Off to the West,"

of impatient speculators and workers flying
to fortune. Alas! their impatience was to be
cooled by a week of isolation on the quarantine station. There was one passenger in
particular whose face is as well known in
Australia as his name, so I need not men-
tion it. He is an expert in mining, and
was sent over by a large syndicate, whose
representatives were no doubt waiting at the
other end of the cable for his report, while
he was rusticating in quarantine. We left
him in his enforced captivity, and when last

CONVALESCENT

seen he was gesticulating and vowing vengeance on the health authorities.

QUARANTINE ISLAND

Prophetically, I picture to myself the saloon passengers so tired of each other in three days that my imaginary sketch, "Quarantine after Three Days," might easily be realized.   Some of our passengers, rather than stay to enjoy the peaceful tranquillity of quarantine, came on in the steamer. Among these were a couple of "Johnnies," that type well known here. They were evidently supplied with more money than brains, and proposed to purchase and float mining properties. If such youths are often entrusted with business of this kind, it is no wonder that bogus mines are often foisted on British investors, and that the latter lose faith in Australian mines.

The question of quarantine is one that creates a vivid impression on the minds of all strangers who happen to encounter it on their first arrival. Having spent five weeks in reaching Australia, they are naturally anxious to land at the earliest opportunity; and when prevented,

"JOHNNIES" FROM HOME.

they are slow to recognise the serious side of the situation, or the wisdom of sacrificing the comfort of the few to the health of the many. We are not all philosophers when our own comfort is at stake. I met one philosopher who had just done a term in quarantine, and he said it was better than living in any hotel in Australia, with the advantage of being free of cost. There was plenty of literature, he said—*Punch* of 1860, *Vanity Fair* of 1870; plenty of objects for study for the naturalist—tarantulas, that sit around the room, and watch you like cricketers in the field; plenty of snakes, too, from five feet long; and crocodiles of alarming aspect. Music was made in that haven of rest by flocks of black cockatoos, screeching in chorus to the energetic solos of the jack-ass. The picture presented by this philosopher made me quite regret to be landed at last on a prosaic jetty at Port Melbourne, instead of being sent to enjoy the hospitality of the West Australian Government in that Eden of the West.

QUARANTINE—AFTER THREE DAYS

A Peep at Albany, West Australia

ALBANY is far from being a fair sample of Australian towns. It is known as "Sleepy Hollow," and bears out its name well, in spite of its increased importance owing to the recent mining boom in West Australia.

I have shown the customary attitude of the Albanians, and it would

"CAB, SIR?"

appear that, presuming that there were some active members of this community once, they have flown to the goldfields, and only left behind the "dead-beats." The solitary case of activity I saw was that of a party of five boys, who had the only cab at the end of the pier, and were loudly soliciting the custom of the arriving travellers. The courage of our party did not rise to trusting our lives to a driver sub-divided into five morsels, so the vociferations of the youngsters were without reward.

A careful survey of the visible specimens of West Australian society leads one to the conclusion that Albany has given way at the knees. The lanky Cornstalk who met the tender was clearly afflicted that way. Then the Dutch-looking gentleman in the *pince-nez* had the same blemish. He was a carter, by the way—think of it, a carter

ALBANY INHABITANTS, AS SEEN FROM THE P. AND O. STEAMBOAT

wearing a *pince-nez*! The row of loafers that I sketched, watching the tender as it arrived—watching, it seemed, for the unwary "new chum"—were also gone at the knees, as must be obvious from my drawing.

Our first sight of "Sleepy Hollow" fully justified its name. On the Parade every seat was occupied by sleepers in all stages of repose, from the deathlike slumber of the person who had evidently been

THE CARMAN WITH THE PINCE-NEZ

making a night of it elsewhere, to the torpor of the rest-weary creature whose natural condition seemed to be an unvarying compromise betwixt waking and sleeping. Some of the weary ones had, however, sufficient energy to crawl across the Parade and watch some Indian jugglers performing outside the hotel.

The police trooper apparently shared the popular aversion to exercise, as, seated at ease on his noble charger, he chatted pleasantly with a kindred lazy citizen. Judging from the proportion of this trooper's anatomy which was utilised in feet, one would suppose that he must be of the mounted infantry order. His appearance recalled an old sketch by John Leech, in *Punch*, of " the footiest man on a horse that was ever seen."

A feature of a visit to Albany is the shipping of gold for London. The gold is packed in wooden boxes and sealed, and an eagle-eyed official accompanies them and sees them securely locked in the bullion room. The mere sight of the outside of the boxes containing such precious freight produces some semblance of eager interest in the bystanders, and they crowd around to catch a glimpse as it comes along on the railway trucks. When the gold is placed on board the tender, we are allowed to go too, but not before. The look on the face of the man at the wheel denotes plainly that he has in his care a charge much more valuable than our poor lives. So stern is the glint in the eye of this son of the brine that it might well strike awe into the heart of the boldest gold-robber and forbid him from plying his trade here.

THE SCENE OUTSIDE THE HOTEL.

One poor mortal, who is seated gazing with hungry eyes at the gold, bears unmistakably in his countenance the crushed and beaten look of the stony-broke. I cannot help wondering whether he is one of those hopeful new arrivals, whom I sketched a few weeks ago, flying off to the goldfields. Perhaps he is one of the poor, over-laden and harassed mil-

SOME ALBANY HORSEMEN

lionaires of these parts. The dead-beat and the millionaire have, after all, much in common—particularly the millionaire.

B

The casual visitor quits Albany without gaining a glimpse of the glory of the Golden West. All the activity is in Perth, to which place all the intercolonial steamers go, as well as some of the vessels from other parts; and, but for the calling of the mail steamers, Albany, one would presume, would scarcely exist at all. The position is, however, one of much importance in a strategic sense, and King George's Sound is well defended.

SHIPPING GOLD

It is well known that the Australians are very particular indeed about the quarantine laws, and great is the anxiety experienced amongst the passengers as the ship approaches St. George's Sound; for those who are desirous of landing at Albany, in order to rush off to seek their fortunes in the mines of Western Australia, are well aware that should there be the slightest symptoms of contagious disease on board, they will be doomed to a prolonged stay, possibly of several weeks' duration, on "Quarantine Island."

Except to those who are anxious to hurry to the mainland, and who consequently resent the delay, there is no very great hardship involved in this compulsory residence.

"Quarantine Island," which is in reality not an island at all, but a peninsula, is at the side of the Bay, and contains a building greatly resembling a small hospital, which is presided over by a Mr. Douglas and his wife, who ably fulfil an arduous position, for not only have they to cater for the stranded passengers, but they have to do their best to pacify and console those who chafe under the restrictions and rules which are necessarily enforced in order to make the isolation efficacious—the most stringent rule, of course, being that which prevents any of the passengers undergoing quarantine from visiting the mainland on any pretext whatever.

GAZING WITH HUNGRY EYES AT THE COLD

Provisions are brought to the "Island" daily in unstinted quantity and of excellent quality, and a safe means of communication exists in the use of the telephone, through which medium both the temporary and habitual residents can converse with their friends on the mainland without the slightest danger of spreading infection.

Students with a taste for natural history will find, as I have noted on an earlier page, much to interest them on the "Island," for not only does it boast of the common or garden spider in considerable quantities, but also the tarantula, snakes, alligators, and black cockatoos—at least, so I am informed. I am also assured that, while fowls and game may be purchased daily from the mainland by those who wish to supplement the *menu* provided by the management, the true sportsman will have no difficulty in bagging a snipe for his breakfast, should he wish for a little sport in the early morning.

Mems. about Melbourne

HOW refreshing, when one walks jaded in the streets of Melbourne, to see all the advertisements on the tram-cars that one can be whisked in a few minutes, and for the modest sum of threepence, to the quietude of the ocean beach. Perhaps the name is a trifle delusive,

BEACONSFIELD PARADE, ST. KILDA

and that particular stretch of sand at South Melbourne somewhat un-romantic; still, we cannot have more for threepence, and that glimpse of Hobson's Bay is cheap at the price.

It is interesting enough, too. There is that bewildering multiplicity of jetties—for what purpose constructed one can only guess—which give to the utilitarian food for speculation, and to the strollers footing for a walk. It may be well known what was the original purpose of these jetties, but to the casual observer they seem only monuments to a past prosperity.

I would suggest that the Beaconsfield Parade be re-christened Bicycle Parade, for the place seems practically given up to wheeldom. I understand that the inhabitants of St. Kilda feel that they miss something when they go inland, away from Hobson's Ocean and its faintly haunting odour. That odour—seaweed and ozone, they say—is apt to drive the more fastidious away from the beach into a bosky solitude of Albert Park. The lake here is an imposing expanse of water ; nay, it is more than that, but

A SHALLOW PRETEXT—ALBERT PARK

I should not like to say how much more—perhaps 60 per cent. water, and the rest "added matter." After the "ocean" at South Melbourne, one expects to have to call this lake a sea at least. There is some good boating carried on here, the density of the water offering no serious impediment to the progress of the craft. A great advantage of this well-conducted sea is in its depth. On a fine summer evening it is crowded with boats, offering infinite chances of disaster ; but the gravest upset on such an occasion would be harmless, except to the clothes, for the—ah—liquid is only about two feet deep, and I picture a shipwreck and its consequences in the sketch, "A Shallow Pretext."

A trip in the opposite direction one day led me to Royal Park, the habitat of all the savage beasts in Victoria. Zoos all over the world are pretty much alike, but the Melbourne Zoo has one striking and original feature which might well be enlarged upon. This is the introduction of wooden beasts, something like Noah's Ark animals in the rough. I have sketched one whose visiting card bears the musical sounding name of Diprotodon Longiceps. To those who have never met this engaging

DIPROTODON LONGICEPS (M'COY)

creature, I ought to explain that it is flat—flat as a flounder—about two inches thick, a mere silhouette. Happily, the original is extinct, otherwise he might rise up and protest against the fun that the scientists of Victoria have poked at him. I know, by the way, that his pet name is M'Coy. It doesn't seem appropriate, somehow.

I think if all the animals were treated in the same way, it might save a lot of trouble, and might make the Zoo more amusing to some, perhaps more terrible to others. I gave a hint in the sketch of the Elephantorum Trunkuli, which seems a pleasing variation on the monotony of original

Jumbos.   I would gladly present the Zoological Society with a model

AT THE ZOO

from this sketch, but I fear it might turn out the White Elephant of the Gardens.

A BIT OF ANCIENT MELBOURNE

I was very anxious to get a sight of ancient Melbourne, but could not find any one to direct me there. One friend told me he had heard of a deserted village, with a town hall given up to rabbits, which he thought was more than ten years old, but this was not what I sought. At last a knowing one hailed me to an out-of-the-way district, where he pointed out a number of houses something like this one, of which I took a note. He said there were some more, but that they had been moved away, all standing, to some township a hundred miles away. I fancy this one refused to be moved, and threatened to lie down. I am still looking for ancient Melbourne.

"OLD TURKEY"

My last mem. is a sketch of an antique party, whom I have named "Old Turkey." He carries about live turkeys for sale, and is a convincing demonstration of the fact that people grow to resemble their most constant associates. His appearance is much more birdlike than his birds.

The Law Courts in Melbourne are the best constructed I have seen; those in Sydney are old-fashioned and the worst. In Melbourne they are airy and light, and at the same time have a style and dignity becoming their use : a richly-polished massive mahogany throne for the judge, nicely arranged seats for the Bar, plenty of room for the public, and, above all, a pleasant little perch for the witness. It has been the custom in Law Courts from the darkest ages to make a witness into a prisoner by torturing him in the courts, not only by the tongue of the cross-examiner, but by the unpleasant position in which witnesses are placed by the architect of the court. The Irish courts are perhaps the most humorous, and at the same time the most awe - inspiring in this matter : there a table is placed in the well of the court, upon which a chair is placed, and the witness has to sit in this chair with his feet on a line with the barristers, with his back either to the jury box or the prisoner; and having got the nervous witness into this most uncomfortable position, he is

A BUNCH OF BARRISTERS

at the mercy of the cross-examiner, who asks him one moment why he does not look at the judge, the next moment why he does not look at him ; rebukes him immediately afterwards for not showing his face to the jury, and then suggests that his evidence cannot be worth much as he is afraid to face the prisoner. By this process the nerves of the strongest witness would break down. Now, in Melbourne, there is a nice little circular stand where a witness can gracefully pose and imagine himself in a Roman Forum of old; certainly he has to be grateful to the designer of the Melbourne courts for giving him an advantage he would not get elsewhere. And Justice Hawkins, had he been in Australia

MR. JUSTICE HOLROYD

instead of England, would not have worried the poor counsel sitting under him into premature age, for he could hardly turn a Melbourne court into the badly ventilated, stifling, unhealthy den he has presided over in the old country.

OLD CHIPS

Perhaps in visiting a Melbourne court one would pay more attention to the courts themselves than to the proceedings, as they happen to be particularly dull and uninteresting. Some case about a cargo of wood brought forward witnesses interesting to the artist as types of good Australian stock. Another case was proceeding about the same time—a dispute among the Oddfellows. It is evident from my sketch that the oddest fellows crowded the court on the occasion. I had not the pleasure of hearing the leader of the Bar,— I might call him the Russell of Australia,— Mr. Purves, but what I did hear of the eloquence of the Bar was enough to show a stranger that they were quite as able as any man

A TIMBER WITNESS

ODDFELLOWS

we have in England, as they made some of the most stupid cases one is likely to meet with entertaining to a marvellous degree.

It may be interesting to members of the Bar to know that I gathered from their brother barristers in Australia that the idea of mixing solicitors' and barristers' practices has been tried in Australia, and with one accord condemned as injurious to both professions.

SOMEBODY IN THE SUPREME COURT

Racing in Australia

ORSE-RACING is certainly one thing which is managed better in Australia than in any other country in the world. It is also safe to say that this sport is better managed at Flemington, the Epsom of Victoria, than anywhere else in Australia.

The differences between the conduct of racing in Australia and in England would take too long to treat fully. In the first place, in England, racing is for racing men, the public being scarcely considered at all. In Australia the racecourse is for the people, and nothing astonishes the stranger more than the perfection of the arrangements for the convenience of the public at Flemington, the scene of the famous Melbourne Cup. Another thing is curious, and that is the quiet and orderly behaviour of the crowd at this racecourse. In fact, apart from racing, it would be difficult to find, all the world over, a better behaved or more interesting crowd.

Taken altogether, the race meetings at Flemington are among the wonders of the world. From the greatest to the smallest detail, nothing which ingenuity can devise or money procure is omitted. To take one

IN THE PADDOCK

YOUNG AUSTRALIA TAKES AN INTEREST

instance, the ladies' boudoirs are as lavishly furnished as the rooms of the finest private houses. The management provide perfumes for general use, and upon the tables are placed cushions with needles, ready threaded

with silk of all colours, so that a lady can sew on a button or put in a stitch in case of an accident to her toilette. Speaking of toilettes, it is generally understood that the annual gathering at the Melbourne Cup is, in point of dress, one of the greatest functions of the world. Magnificent as is the accommodation for the " classes," however, the masses are equally well provided for. Behind the grand-stand the hill rises and affords a view of the course. Upon this there is a garden which any English squire might envy. Here the humbler folk can "camp

AN OLD STARTER AT FLEMINGTON

out" with their picnic baskets and enjoy themselves to their hearts' content. Boiling water is supplied, so that they can have tea in their own way without expense. This garden is picturesque and wild, as though Nature had made it, and gives no uncomfortable suggestion of a need to "keep off the grass"; at the same time it is perfectly planted and kept, and is altogether an ideal retreat. At the back of the grand-stand are huge letters of the alphabet, placed at equal distances —this is one more of the many happy thoughts of the secretary for the comfort of the public. The intention is to provide readily dis-

THE PEOPLE'S GARDEN

THE STARTING MACHINE

tinguishable landmarks for people who wish to appoint a meeting place for friends. An appointment to meet at a given hour at A, B, or C, avoids all confusion which might arise from naming a less definite trysting place.

The train service at Flemington is admirably managed. There are different exits for different parts of the course, and when returning, only sufficient people to fill one train are allowed on the platform at once. You take your seats in comfort, without any rush or crush. As soon as one train moves off another is ready, and every one gets away without the least inconvenience.

Coming to the management of the course and the racing, there are several points upon which the Australian institution is much better conducted than similar places elsewhere. The "starting gate" is a remarkable innovation and works to perfection. The use of this invention does away with all the tricks of jockeys, by which some make false starts purposely to fret and tire the cracks. The difference between a start with the gate and one without it is great. The regularity and machine-like promptitude of the one, as seen in Australia, makes the start on the old system, still in vogue in England, look ridiculous. Considering the long delays and unsatisfactory starts which the English custom involves, and the frequent appeals to the committee against jockeys, it will not be surprising if the system is adopted at home. I have sketched the clerk of the course on his white charger—an old-time racer, I understand—engaged in superintending a start. As the horses cannot pass the "gate" until it is raised, there is no possibility of any obstreperous ones breaking away. It might be supposed that there would be some difficulty in getting horses to face this strange object, but there is hardly any objection on this score, horses readily getting used to it.

In another sketch I show Mr. George Watson, who has officiated

c

THE BRITISH METHOD OF STARTING
THE AUSTRALIAN METHOD

THE FENCE IN ENGLAND
THE FENCE IN AUSTRALIA

A STUDY IN CONTRASTS

as starter at Flemington for many years. When I saw this veteran he was sitting in the weighing room, having been invalided, and obliged for a while to forego his accustomed duties.

THE CLERK OF THE COURSE

Some of the bookmakers of Melbourne have physiognomies sufficiently striking to attract observation, though it would be flattery to designate them as personally attractive. It is otherwise with the ladies, and it is somewhat of a surprise to a stranger to see fashionably-dressed ladies walking about the paddock unattended, admiring the horses and comparing notes, a thing which in England would be considered impossible. But then it must be remembered that every aspect of the pastime is different in the two countries, and generally the advantage is greatly in

AUSTRALIAN BOOKMAKERS

favour of Australia. In England there is a disgraceful disregard of public convenience, and, whereas from an Australian meeting you return home as spick and span as you left, in England you are lucky if you reach home without having your clothes torn off your backs, ladies in particular finding the ordeal extremely trying. In England the course is a pandemonium, the rough element dominating the situation. In Australia, to a great extent, this element is absent.

Yet another difference in the actual racing is found in the sensational nature of Australian steeplechasing as compared with the same sport in England. Stiff fences and huge stone walls are fixed on the Australian courses, and the way in which the riders go at these formidable obstacles is sensational and the results often startling. Fatal accidents to horses are of quite frequent occurrence, and not a few jockeys are killed outright or maimed for life, while severe falls with more fortunate endings are so numerous as to excite no notice whatever. It is well known that a famous Australian jumper, racing in England, failed to obtain a place in any of the chief contests simply because he lost time and labour in jumping high over his obstacles, not understanding a fence which is constructed to suit horses which can run but not jump.

The universality of the interest taken in racing in Australia is certainly conspicuous. Every one goes to most of the chief races, and it is considered quite an ordinary thing for ladies to bet on the course. Young people also appear to take an absorbing interest in the sport, and not unfrequently are seen indulging in the ruling passion for backing the winner.

A Suburban Race Meeting

A FEW NOTES IN THE CROWD

ONE thing which immediately strikes a stranger visiting the race-courses in Australia is that, while in England racing is carried on in the first place by and for owners and trainers, and the

AMONG THE BOOKIES

public entertainment is the secondary consideration, in Australia the public is the first consideration. This catering for the public is carried to per-

A BOOKIE'S HAT

fection at Flemington. I went, however, a few days ago to a suburban race meeting of a different class, and paid my two shillings to mingle with the crowd. At this place the "bookies" adopt much more extravagant methods of advertisement than at Flemington; one in particular attracted my attention with a wonderful hat labelled all over "double event." It was interesting to note that among the crowd were husbands and wives debating about their investments in the ring. Here were elderly respectable labouring people, some seemingly past the three score and ten, displaying keen zest in the proceedings. Boys, almost children, astonished me by their conversation. They appeared thoroughly familiar with the intricacies of the betting-ring, and were wagering away their weekly pence with the recklessness of a plunger. Some of these youngsters I saw scrambling up the wire netting which divided the crowd from the course at one point. From this coign of vantage they called out encouragements and criticisms to the jockeys as they passed, showing that they were no strangers in these parts. I noted that a portion of the ground immediately abutting on the course seemed part of a farm, and its appearance gave

YOUNG SPORTSMEN

a rural picturesqueness to the scene. Racing touts of maturer years se-
lected a spot far from the madding crowd to get a word with the

CLOSE TIME

jockeys as they passed on their preliminary canter before the race. The
questions asked seemed innocent enough, but were intended to elicit
something in shape of a tip at the eleventh hour.
The youth who asked his friend in the saddle,
"What are you on, Bill?" is not, as one might
fancy, inquiring the name of his mount.

An extraordinary sight at this meeting was
to see some thousands of hares, more or less
tame, in the centre of the course, huddled together in batches. They had a good view of the
racing, but they have soon to take part in a
more serious race—a race for life in the cours-
ing season, as I understand they are preserved
for that purpose.

AFTER A STEEPLECHASE

In the steeplechases we had the usual mishaps—a few horses killed
and a jockey or two injured. The pluck and dash shown in these races
make a stranger wonder that a jockey is ever left intact at the winning

"WHAT ARE YOU ON, BILL?"

BETWEEN THE EVENTS

post. As it is, I notice a jockey arriving after a race with his boot off and his jacket in tatters. He cheerily salutes a brother jockey, who is just convalescent and hobbles about with a stick, and jokes pass about the latest spill, showing that these hardy fellows enjoy the humour of their mishaps, and make light of their perils.

Side-Lights on Sydney

SYDNEY, so old-fash-
ioned in everything,
curiously enough has
either never adopted, or if it
has, has discarded the old-
fashioned Barrister's Wig for
the Speaker of its Parliament.
This is a pity, for it struck
me forcibly that if ever a
Speaker wanted a wig, it was
the presiding genius over all
the debates in Sydney. Not
only did his " dome of thought
want re-thatching," but his
spacious neck seemed as if a
little horse-hair would have
saved him from the draughts
of the open doors, which
flapped to and fro on either
side of the chair ; the gown

THE SPEAKER

was all right, but the knee-breeches and the buckle shoes and the wig
were missing. The Sergeant-at-Arms—a handsome old gentleman—who

looked the part down to the waist with his cut-away coat and his frill, was but a commonplace individual so far as his legs were concerned. Where were the knee-breeches, the silk stockings, and the buckles? In fact, looking over these few sketches I made in my first walk through Sydney, it will be observed there is a total absence of dignity and that

A WELL-KNOWN FIGURE

A MEMBER OF THE OPPOSITION

picturesqueness of figure always attributed to the Australian until one sees him at home. The Police Constable, for instance, has hardly the figure one would imagine excessive horse exercise would allow to remain, and from the huge whip he carries in his hand, one must believe that he still keeps true to Australian habits by living on horseback. A member of the Opposition surely neither rides nor cycles to the Parliament

House; and judging from the statues, the best type of Sydney men must have been of the same order, or else the sculptors of Australia have done a serious injustice to its great men. I select the "Dalley" statue. Who could believe that this gentleman was ever a fiery orator or a leader of men. But after all the harbour in Sydney is considered so beautiful that it more than makes amends for any inartistic drawbacks the town may possess.

THE DALLEY STATUE

Mems. in Sydney

THE Sydney Law Courts are cramped and old-fashioned. I visited the Divorce Court, my attention having been directed to it through reading that a "record" had just been made in the number of cases polished off at one sitting. Matrimonial suits are tried in a room about as large as a packing-case, where people have to walk on one another when they move about. The cases tumble over one another with just as little ceremony, and are disposed of at the rate of nineteen a day ; at least that, I understand, is the record recently put up. I should think this beats Chicago, where liberated spouses are turned out by machinery.

As I left, I noticed a typical "sundowner," who had been looking in at the proceedings. I asked him if he was looking for work. The eloquence of his silence, and the speaking blank-

A "SUNDOWNER"

ness of his look, I shall not easily forget. He stood transfixed while I made this note, and he had not found a word to express his sentiments when I left.

THE SYDNEY DIVORCE COURT

" The Domain," Sydney

THE "larrikin" has been described before as being one of the lowest types of humanity in the Colonies ; yet he does not look it, and there is another phase of low life which does not assume its correct *rôle* either. The "sundowner"—another name for the Sydney tramp—appears a greater ruffian than the larrikin, yet in many respects he is his superior. He is a loafer, not a sneak ; an idle, worthless, drunken ne'er-do-well, perhaps, but not the crafty, bullying blackguard that the larrikin is.

There possibly may be amongst the sundowners many respectable but unfortunate citizens, driven through dire necessity to make their home in the Domain ; but it is when you get the mixture of larrikin

NEWSPAPER PYJAMAS

and sundowner that the very lowest type of character is obtained. In the sketch we have a horde of these ruffians stealthily creeping up in the twilight to worry and blackmail the innocent young lovers on the stone seat— doubtless fresh arrivals from the Old Country, continuing a flirtation begun on the steamer, where as fellow-passengers they have been thrown into each other's society for the past six or seven weeks. They are whispering vows of eternal fidelity, and so rapt are they in their mutual admiration, that they are

A LOVERS' MEETING

oblivious of the approach of the wretches who make the Domain their happy hunting-ground from sunset to dawn.

In the daytime, like the bats and owls, they vanish and keep in hiding, and then respectable people may enjoy the beautiful walks in the park and about the Government House unmolested, and with their children and friends enjoy the beautiful and picturesque scenery with which the Domain abounds.

The view of the harbour and the shipping is particularly animated and interesting, and there are many natural beauties to be observed in the park itself, which deserve more than a passing notice. Amongst other natural curiosities in one of the side paths are to be observed a group

IN THE DOMAIN

of rocks eaten away by the changing tides till they resemble nothing so much as a number of strange and uncouth monsters of a bygone age—at any rate, thus they were regarded by a lady and her charge who were admiring them on the day of my visit.

Although the larrikin and the sundowner may not be rampant in the daytime, the Domain is not altogether free from an element of peril and danger of another kind. It is well known how important a

D

A FREE-AND-EASY GALLOP

part the horse plays in the every-day life of the Australian, and in this park the horses are allowed to graze at their own sweet will. Being very high-spirited animals and full of fun, there is quite an excitement when their owners come to capture them after having been loose all day. In stating that the accompanying sketch was drawn from

A CHARACTERISTIC SPOT

nature on the spot, it is necessary to explain (lest he should be accused of maligning the magnificent horses of Australia) that the artist was so disconcerted at the wild careering of the animals that he was unable to do justice to the drawing, although the native Australians seemed to regard the whole affair as a matter of course, and sat about on the grass quite undisturbed at the proximity of the horses' heels.

As the sun sets, and the better class of visitors to the Domain retire, the park becomes the undisputed property of the loafers and sundowners, who nightly use the niches and crevices of the rocks as their dormitories, from the dim recesses of which they draw forth their

MORNING ABLUTIONS

"bed-clothes," consisting of old newspapers and wrappers. Observe the gentleman in the sketch carefully adjusting his newspaper pyjamas and tying up himself in a weird fashion—thus literally becoming "wrapped in literature."

In the morning these gentry perform their ablutions in the cattle troughs abounding in the park, and later on may be seen fishing for their breakfasts from the wooden piles in the harbour. They are sometimes fortunate enough to catch a sufficient number of fish to sell for a few pence, and thus provide themselves with food for the remainder of the day, till darkness once more drives them to their primitive resting-places. All tell the same tale : they were born tired, and have never been able to throw off the feeling.

It seems to the stranger a shame that the best parts of a beautiful park like the Domain should be given up to these vagrants, and that better regulations are not enforced to protect what might be made one of the most beautiful places of public recreation in the world, possessing as it does so many natural facilities and advantages. A strong hand is required to deal effectively with this difficult problem.

WAITING

Character Sketches in Sydney

SYDNEY on a Saturday night is a good deal like many another city; most of its aspects are squalid and far from pleasing. In "Paddy's Market" we see gathered together a crowd which would not be out of place in the East end of London, although, on the whole, the Sydney crowd is less noisy and less good-tempered. Brawls are not frequent, but there is little of breezy good nature about these people. If they are enjoying themselves, they do not exhibit many outward signs of their gaiety. In this market the Jew cheap clothes sellers keep up the resemblance to the East end, adhering to that seductively aggressive manner which stamps their kind all the world over. Stalls with cheap lithographs, music, china and fancy goods, are

ranged side by side with the stands of venders of sweetstuffs, fruit and
vegetables, fried potatoes and poultry, the last, which are "alive, alive!"
adding to the confusion of sounds with their unmelodious cries. Outside
the market, about the street corners, it is interesting to watch the
groups around the street preachers, who hold forth in the lurid glare of
a flaring oil lamp. The discussion on theology which takes place after-

SATURDAY NIGHT

SUNDAY MORNING

wards would be amusing but for the seriousness of its subject—the
opinions are so free and various, and the arguments so highly coloured.
As a contrast, there are the larger groups of people congregated in the
courts leading out of the chief streets of the city, where betting and
gambling are freely carried on as a regular thing. Here you find
tradesmen, clerks, and scores of nondescripts of the lower orders,

together with a fair sprinkling of larrikins, and the conduct of these crowds is, as may be imagined, far from edifying.

In any Sunday crowd the larrikin is always conspicuous, and no description of this city has ever been attempted without including the larrikin. It is difficult to speak of this social excrescence without being harsh. Most people unfamiliar with Australia are apt to suppose that the larrikin is merely the Antipodean "'Arry." This is not so at all.

STREET LARRIKINS

'Arry is sublimely innocent of criminal instincts; he is generally a hard-working tradesman—a coster for choice—and his ambition is to marry his "donah" and achieve a decent ideal of domestic felicity. The familiar "coster" songs are, as a rule, true to nature, and depict the London 'Arry with fidelity. It is true that the larrikin has his prototype in other countries, but in European and American cities he is merely a representative of the criminal classes, and as such he is held in subjection by the police. In Sydney he is a "chartered

libertine," and suffers little molestation from the law, though he freely
molests law-abiding citizens.   Individually, he is a low, loafing sneak
and a thorough coward.   Collectively, the " Glebe push," the " Rock
push," the "Argyle Cut push," and other gangs are the terrors of the

OUTSIDE PADDY'S MARKET

streets after dark.   The larrikin has nothing manly about him.   He is a
sharp, active, horsey-looking, vicious cad ; he very rarely does any work,
but mostly lives upon the lowest means possible—by the vice of others.

The "larrikinesses" are melancholy creatures. One wonders what their mothers could have been. About their outward appearance there is some resemblance to "'Arriet" of Cockaigne. They affect large hats and feathers and gaudy colours and their ways are "loud." But poor 'Arriet, with all her vulgarity and sometimes rowdy ways, has a sturdy

STREET GAMBLING

virtue and independence which are altogether admirable; and she is invariably a hard-working girl, and often thrifty, except in the matter of feathers. The larrikiness sometimes works; often she lives by bullying her parents and compelling them to support her and her low companions. Many of these creatures of both sexes are very young, and a

THE YOUTHFUL LARRIKIN

glance at any of them shows clearly the immature criminal, and also, alas! that for such there can be no future but that of social pests and vermin. This feature is the darkest blot upon Australian society, and upon Sydney in particular. It is strange that, with an immense body of clerical and lay workers in every branch of mission work, this evil should be so rampant and unchecked. Yet it is said that, in times past, the state of things in this particular was much worse; this seems, to a stranger, barely credible.

PADDY'S MARKET

Manly : The Brighton of Australia

MANLY BEACH is known as the Brighton of Australia. Why it should be so called is a mystery ; for though the trip by steamer across Sydney Harbour to Manly is really beautiful, there is no more resemblance between Manly and our Brighton than between Sydney Harbour and the Grand Canal. London-by-the-Sea, as Brighton is often called, possesses no naturally attractive features. It is simply a city by the sea, whereas Manly is topographically picturesque, boasting of excellent cliffs and a good sea front. The arrangements upon its beach, however, are worthy of a pantomime. There is a row of structures resembling sheep-pens, each one of which encloses some presumably valuable, though diminutive, botanical treasure. These are arrayed in a painfully straight line, and are flanked by an equally rigid line of toy Noah's-Ark-like fir trees. Grass grows near the

AN ARTISTIC LANDLORD

beach, which is tastefully decorated with broken bottles, thoughtfully left behind by kind-hearted beanfeasters.

The only point of similarity between our seaside resort and Manly is the large flock of itinerant photographers that flourish at both places, and here they seem to thrive well upon Australian vanity. I saw Manly in the winter, but undoubtedly it is most popular during the

SOME CLERICS

summer season, and the place appears to be well suited to the crowd who fly thither to escape the heat of Sydney.

Looking eastward from the beach, the cliffs are surmounted by a Catholic college, presided over by a celebrated Australian cardinal. On the occasion of my visit the beach below seemed to be reserved for clerical visitors, who had evidently been paying their respects to the cardinal, and who were now discussing Church matters by the sad sea waves.

About ten or twelve miles along the coast is a fine hotel, the enterprising proprietor of which runs vehicles, for the convenience of tourists, from Manly to his establishment and back. It is well worth the journey, if only for the sake of the drive, which is through interesting bush scenery, opening out upon a bold sea front, while at the

ON THE BOAT

hotel the landlord offers further picturesque attractions in the shape of mural decorations of a somewhat remarkable character. A Frenchman is this courteous host, with decidedly artistic tastes—or, shall I say, energy—for he has covered his walls with paintings in oil—replicas of well-known pictures, which have reached him through the medium of the coloured supplements to the illustrated papers. The pictures resemble frescoes, and have lost nothing of their brilliant colouring in the copying process. If monsieur the artist is modest and cares not to dilate upon his work, madame is always ready to act as cicerone and expatiate upon the beauties of the artist-proprietor's self-apportioned labours while the *déjeûner* is being prepared. The latter is certain to

ON THE BEACH

be excellent, and will be particularly gratifying after the long journey. The meal ended, the gardens will well repay a visit, containing as they do quite a menagerie of native and foreign birds and animals, while the curious little Australian bears, asleep in all sorts of attitudes in the trees of the gardens, are certain to evoke a great deal of interest. These harmless and docile little animals are very tame and inoffensive, and so lazy that they will scarcely move if a bird settles upon them, as is frequently the case. It is very curious to notice how they stow themselves away in the forked branches of the trees, and adapt themselves to the apparently uncomfortable positions which they are forced to assume.

A VISITOR FROM ALBANY

ON THE BOAT: AN IRISHMAN

Driving back, one is shown a gaunt-looking shell of a house, which is reputed to be haunted; and the thought is impressed upon one's mind that it can no longer be said of Australia, as of America, that the country is too young to be able to possess a ghost. The steamers

THE HAUNTED HOUSE

which ply between Manly and Sydney present all the features of the small steamers to be seen on the Thames; and the scene on the deck of one of these Antipodean small craft is one which might be witnessed on any summer's day at Gravesend or Greenwich, save for the fact that here the garb of the mounted police is rather more picturesque than that of Tommy Atkins, and that the Irish element is rather more in evidence. The son of Erin depicted in the sketch is evidently ruminating, as he gazes across the harbour, upon the hardships which befell his ancestors in these same waters many years gone by. As the steamer passes the heads of the harbour the sea becomes boisterous as in the Atlantic.

THE AUSTRALIAN BEAR

A Visit to Adelaide

NGLING on the jetty is an exciting sport, and there must be something heroic in the composition of the anglers of Australia, for here at Largs they ply their sport regardless of the screeching puff-puff. They may be run over and lose life or limb, but they go on angling just the same.

I have sketched the driver and fireman of the engine, resigned to the impossibility of clearing the line of prostrate fishermen, giving in to the popular passion and doing a cast or two on their own account.

At Port Melbourne the same infatuated self-devotion is observable. On the railway pier enthusiastic followers of Izaak Walton sit all day long, unmindful of the trains, which nearly push them off into the sea. The hawsers of the mail steamers may decapitate them, or whirl them away in fragments—their enthusiasm suffers no abatement. In Sydney, also, anglers will sit over the water while the sharks nibble at their toes; they do not care so long as they get a bite. This fervour would not be surprising if Australian fish were worth catching, but they are not. They are of different shapes and sizes, and have various misleading names; but, as far as eating goes, they are all alike—flavourless, coarse, and dry.

AN "AGENT"

E

Adelaide is a bright, cheerful city, very prettily situated on a small plateau raised above the general level of the plain which stretches from the foot of the hills to the shore of St. Vincent's Gulf. Adelaide is modest, and does not compete with Melbourne and Sydney. Melbourne is proud of its fine streets and its trams, Sydney of its harbour, but Adelaide " blows " about nothing. Still, Adelaide has its " brick-fielder,"

FISHING EXTRAORDINARY

which blows like all creation. This is the north wind, which comes down hot off the centre of the continent and carries all before it. In a north wind Adelaide's modesty is so apparent that you can see nothing else ; she is veiled in an impenetrable mist of sand, pebbles, waste-paper, and other unconsidered trifles.

Adelaide on wheels is a curious study. The tramcars are all drawn by horses, and are of the old American pattern, with top seats and an awning, the latter giving a very cumbersome look, especially in a gale

of wind. The mail coaches are
extremely ancient, ugly, and noisy,
most of them dating from the
early days when they were built
to stand the rough wear of bush
roads ; consequently they are in-
destructible. I have sketched one
of these conveyances in a dust
storm as I saw it, with an unfortunate gentleman alone in a pri-

A DUSTY DAY

vileged seat on top. There is another conveyance called a "carette,"
which is the wonder of this city, to which it is peculiar. It is like a
piece of a railway carriage tacked on to the outside platform of a
tramcar, the whole running on small wheels, which increase the appearance of heaviness and clumsiness. These vehicles are a comparatively
new invention, though their appearance suggests a survival from last
century.

A SKETCH IN THE POST-OFFICE

In nearly all
Australian cities the
post-office is the
most important build-
ing. Adelaide is no
exception to this rule.
The stranger in
search of the inter-
esting is sent to the
post-office first of all.
It is a fine building,
out of all proportion

to the size of the city. The central hall is an excellent place in which to study character. Here, all letters addressed to the post-office, and all unclaimed letters, are tabulated alphabetically, the names of addressees being placed in frames on screens, where any one may inspect them. Here come the "new chum"—a rather rare creature now—to look for letters from "home"; the feckless "remittance man," to see if that letter "with enclosure" has arrived; the widow, anxious for news from the relatives of the late lamented; the old identity, whose daily task it is to come and scan this board, vaguely expecting, like Mr. Micawber, that something will "turn up." All these and many other characters come in hope of finding their names on the board, and while some may be seen to leave in various stages of the dejection of "hope deferred," others rush off to the delivery window and eagerly demand the expected letter. I noticed one man who went through all the names

STATUE OF ROBERT BURNS—ONE LEG UP TO DATE!

on the board, and now and then made a note of some name. I was informed that this was an "agent," who made small "commissions" by informing people who could not read, or who are unable to go to the post-office, when letters are awaiting them.

North Terrace is a pretty boulevard, though not sufficiently patronised by the Adelaide gentry, who seem to prefer Rundle Street, with its narrow footways and miscellaneous shops, as a place for promenading. Strolling along North Terrace, I came on Robert Burns, "presented to the city by the South Australian Caledonian Society."

It is a speaking likeness of the poet, who seems to be complaining that they have put him into striped trousers, one leg of which he has torn off in his rage. Walking round to observe the expression of the angered poet, I found him wearing the usual complacent smile, and not trousers at all. The effect from the back is caused by a pillar placed behind the poet to support him. It was unkind of the Adelaide Caledonians to provide this reminder that their national poet frequently needed the aid of some such visible means of support.

On North Terrace the ministers of religion mostly seem to meet, probably on their way to or from the public library. I sketched a typical group, and should gather that, as a rule, the lot of a colonial divine is not a hard one ; those seen about the towns do not give the impression of overwork. At the same time, I am told that often the ministers in country districts have very hard times, as they have to travel great distances to fulfil their duties, and often have very small stipends.

CLERICAL TYPES IN ADELAIDE

In Adelaide a large number of people appear to live all day in the streets. Many of these are bookmakers, and jobbers in mining shares and their clients; the rest seem to be made up of country people and loafers. The note of the loafer in these parts is independence ; he is

THE MARKET GARDENER

never looking for a job, but he is not above taking an occasional contract for "deep-sinking" at an adjacent bar. One type, which the most hasty traveller cannot miss in any part of Australia, is the Chinese market gardener. He is a thrifty, peaceable creature, who works hard and lives anyhow, and finally returns to China to live on his savings. Chinese women are not allowed to immigrate, hence "John" does not multiply; also, the number of Chinamen permitted to land is strictly limited, though few people would vote for the total exclusion of these Celestial visitants.

ADELAIDE TYPES

Football Notes

I AM quite prepared to be told that these caricatures of Australian footballers, my first impressions after seeing an hour's play, are libels on the famous athletes of the country. Out of the many thousands who go to sports of this kind, probably not twenty go with the object of seeing the humorous side of it. All are terribly serious. Their thick-necked, long-bodied, bandy-legged Herculean cousin is, in their eyes, a perfect Adonis. Their long, lanky, favourite, all bone and sinew, is, in their eyes, an Apollo Belvidere. In fact, in every case they merely look through glasses of sportsmen, admiring the speed and cleverness of their favourites, not thinking of onlooking for the artistic effect; and when they see their champion depicted, as seen through the microscope of the caricaturist, they are naturally surprised and incredulous. I do not expect Australians to be different in this respect from other nationalities. An exception, by the way, I found,

A GOOD RUN

strange to say, among the sensitive Americans, when I gave my first
impressions of their football, a game in which there is more science
than in all other football systems in the world put together—a game
in which fatalities are numerous, and is played with a seriousness and
intenseness unsurpassed in any game I have ever seen.   The players
I have seen depicted in pictures compared with gladiators in the

THE UMPIRE'S LOT IS NOT
A HAPPY ONE

Roman amphitheatre, yet a more ridiculous, grotesque, pantomimic
crowd, on the field, it has never been one's lot to see.   Long massive
hair, falling all over the head; huge india-rubber shields on the noses;
extraordinary shapeless garments padded all over; shields on the legs,
on the fingers; pads on the heads; protections on the ears—nothing
could be more absurd; yet to their public they are Adonises and
Apolloes.   There is as much difference between the Victorian and

READY TO START

American game of football as there is in the costume worn by the players. I notice the Victorians are attired above the waist as scullers in a boat-race, and from that down they have loose kind of garments cut below the knee; stockings and boots, seemingly not protected in any way. When I saw the game, some of these stockings slipped down, and the players wore wide - awake hats, and other caps, which fell off in the scrimmage, al-though most of the players are bareheaded, with short cropped hair. As regards the game it-self, I can only say that

SCORING-BOARD

I was too busy in picking out the most ludicrous on the field—the duty of the caricaturist—rather than in watching the play.   But what

SIGNALLING A GOAL

I saw of it struck me as the fastest game I have ever seen.   Hands are used, legs, heads, everything, in breaking down all the rules of

other football systems, with the one object of speed. Science must
therefore to a great extent suffer. Every man seems to play his best
individually. The combination is nothing compared with the

A THROW IN

combination in any other football I have seen; although, no doubt, it
exists. The science of the Victorian game of football may be too
quick for a stranger to grasp at first sight, or an artist to depict with
justice.

Butler & Tanner, The Selwood Printing Works, Frome, and London.

Novels by ...

...Guy Boothby

SPECIAL AND ORIGINAL DESIGNS.

Each volume attractively illustrated by Stanley L. Wood and others.

Crown 8vo, cloth gilt, trimmed edges, **5s.**

Mr. RUDYARD KIPLING says:--

"Mr. GUY BOOTHBY has come to great honours now. His name is large upon hoardings, his books sell like hot cakes, and he keeps a level head through it all. I've met him several times in England, and he added to my already large respect for him."

PHAROS, THE EGYPTIAN.

"This powerful novel is weird, wonderful, and soul-thrilling. Mr. BOOTHBY succeeds in making it almost real, and its marvels and mysteries almost credible. There never was in this world so strange and wonderful a love story, and Mr. GUY BOOTHBY's admirers will probably agree that the most marvellous fiction he has ever produced is 'Pharos, the Egyptian.'"—*The Scotsman.*

ACROSS THE WORLD FOR A WIFE.

THE LUST OF HATE.

BUSHIGRAMS.

THE FASCINATION OF THE KING.

DR. NIKOLA.

THE BEAUTIFUL WHITE DEVIL.

A BID FOR FORTUNE; Or, Dr. Nikola's Vendetta.

IN STRANGE COMPANY: A Story of Chili and the Southern Seas.

THE MARRIAGE OF ESTHER: A Torres Straits Sketch.

LONDON: WARD, LOCK & CO., LIMITED

NEW COMPLETE LIBRARY EDITION OF

G. J. Whyte=Melville's Novels

Large Crown 8vo, cloth gilt, **3s. 6d.** *per volume.*

THE late G. J. WHYTE-MELVILLE, uniting, as he did, the qualities of poet, novelist, sportsman, and leader of society, has long been acknowledged to stand above rivalry when dealing with sport and the romance of old. Although the sale of his works has always been large, the publishers feel that the time has now arrived to issue an edition more worthy of his fame, and have therefore pleasure in announcing a monthly issue of his novels, complete in about twenty-five volumes. Each volume will be illustrated by front-rank artists, well printed from type specially cast, on best antique paper, and neatly and handsomely bound in cloth gilt.

1. **KATERFELTO: A Story of Exmoor.**
   With Four Illustrations by LUCY E. KEMP-WELCH.

2. **CERISE: A Tale of the Last Century.**
   With Four Illustrations by G. P. JACOMB-HOOD.

3. **SARCHEDON: A Legend of the Great Queen.**
   With Four Illustrations by S. E. WALLER.

4. **SONGS AND VERSES, and THE TRUE CROSS.**
   With Five Illustrations by S. E. WALLER.

5. **MARKET HARBOROUGH, and INSIDE THE BAR.**
   With Four Illustrations by JOHN CHARLTON.

6. **BLACK BUT COMELY: The Adventures of Jane Lee.**
   With Four Illustrations by S. E. WALLER.

7. **ROSINE, AND SISTER LOUISE.**
   With Four Illustrations by G. P. JACOMB-HOOD.

8. **KATE COVENTRY.**
   With Four Illustrations by LUCY E. KEMP-WELCH.

9. **ROY'S WIFE.**
   With Four Illustrations by G. P. JACOMB-HOOD.

10. **THE GLADIATORS: A Tale of Rome and Judæa.**
    With Four Illustrations by J. AMBROSE WALTON.

11. **HOLMBY HOUSE: A Tale of Old Northamptonshire.**
    With Four Illustrations by LUCY E. KEMP-WELCH.

LONDON: WARD, LOCK & CO., LIMITED.

NEW LIBRARY EDITION OF

Henry Kingsley's Novels.

EDITED BY CLEMENT K. SHORTER.

Well printed on good paper, from type specially cast. Neatly and handsomely bound. Illustrated by eminent artists. Cloth gilt, **3s. 6d.** *per volume.*

1. ## THE RECOLLECTIONS OF GEOFFRY HAMLYN.
   With a Photogravure Portrait of Henry Kingsley, and a Memoir by CLEMENT K. SHORTER. Illustrated by HERBERT RAILTON.

2. ## RAVENSHOE.
   With Frontispiece by R. CATON WOODVILLE.

3. ## THE HILLYARS AND THE BURTONS.
   With a Note on Old Chelsea Church by CLEMENT K. SHORTER. Illustrated by HERBERT RAILTON.

4. ## SILCOTE OF SILCOTES.
   With Frontispiece by LANCELOT SPEED.

5. ## STRETTON.
   With Frontispiece by GEORGE M. HENTON.

6. ## AUSTIN ELLIOT, and THE HARVEYS.
   With Frontispiece by WALTER PAGET.

7. ## MDLLE. MATHILDE.
   With Frontispiece by HOLLAND TRINGHAM.

8. ## OLD MARGARET, and other Stories.
   With a Frontispiece by ROBERT SAUBER.

9. ## VALENTIN, and NUMBER SEVENTEEN.
   With a Frontispiece by R. CATON WOODVILLE.

10. ## OAKSHOTT CASTLE, and THE GRANGE GARDEN.
    With a Frontispiece by W. H. OVEREND.

11. ## REGINALD HETHEREGE, and LEIGHTON COURT.
    With a Frontispiece by GORDON BROWNE.

12. ## THE BOY IN GREY, and other Stories.
    With a Frontispiece by A. FORESTIER.

LONDON : WARD, LOCK & CO., LIMITED.

3

Works by Ethel Turner

(Mrs. H. R. CURLEWIS).

Crown 8vo, cloth gilt, bevelled boards, gilt edges, **3s. 6d.** *each.*

"Miss Ethel Turner is Miss Alcott's true successor. The same healthy, spirited tone is visible which girls and boys recognised and were grateful for in 'Little Women' and 'Little Men,' the same absence of primness, and the same love of adventure."—*The Bookman.*

THE CAMP AT WANDINONG.
Illustrated by FRANCES EWAN and others.

MISS BOBBIE.
Illustrated by HAROLD COPPING.

THE LITTLE LARRIKIN.
Illustrated by A. J. JOHNSON.

SEVEN LITTLE AUSTRALIANS.
Illustrated by A. J. JOHNSON.

THE FAMILY AT MISRULE.
A SEQUEL TO THE ABOVE.
Illustrated by A. J. JOHNSON.

Square Fcap. 8vo, cloth elegant, gilt top, **2s. 6d.** *each.*

THE STORY OF A BABY.
Illustrated by ST. CLAIR SIMMONS.

THE LITTLE DUCHESS, and other Stories.
Illustrated by SYDNEY COWELL.

LONDON: WARD, LOCK & CO., LIMITED.

www.ingramcontent.com/pod-product-compliance
Lightning Source LLC
Chambersburg PA
CBHW030009030726
47499CB00008B/2972